Published by Insights Press, Rochester, Minnesota.

Printed in the United States of America

Mitch Anthony's books are available at special quantity discounts. For more information, please contact
(507) 282-2723 or orders@mitchanthony.com

www.mitchanthony.com

Managing Editor: Debbie Anthony
Interior Design: Greg Wimmer
Cover Design: Greg Wimmer

ISBN: 978-0-9727523-5-0

D0312950

The CASH IN THE HAT

by Mitch Anthony

Illustrated by Greg Wimmer

When you go to work
they give you cash

You try real hard
to make it last.

If you earn four
but just spend two
There's some for bills
and some for you.

If cash you have
you'll need a hat
To use some day
for this and that.

The hat must be round
and big enough
To save for clothes
and trips and stuff.

If you take some out
then put more back

For if you don't
it won't stay black.

When you
take out three
to go to the store

Then go to work
and put back four.

If you see a thing
that you
want now

REACH IN

THE HAT

And take cash out.

If the cash is gone
you'll have to wait

Which you won't like
which you will hate!

You may see a house
you want to own

And talk to a bank
and get a loan.

This house you like
but it feels too small

You want a house
that's big and tall.

You call the bank
for one more loan

You want
a big house
you can own.

You borrow more
and have less cash

You must buy chairs
you must buy gas!

And a big
green
lawn.

Your hat is empty
your cash is gone

You have a
big house

Then one day
you lose your hat
There's no more cash
and that is that.

The empty hat
will turn to red

The hat is sad
it needs a head.

In your mail
you'll find a card
That sends you cash
a whole new start.

You use the card
and buy some stuff
You buy some more
it's not enough.

You buy
and buy
with your
shiny cards

You don't have to wait
it's not too hard.

You buy it now
you buy it all

You buy new things
at the new mall.

More magic cards
come to your door

First one, then two,
then three, then four.

The more you spend
the more you get

Now you have stuff
now you have debt.

What is debt?
you will ask.

You ask your dog
you ask your cat.

But if you're smart
you'll ask your hat.

It's like mud
that drags you down.

It's like bees
that chase you 'round.

What is DEBT?

Meow

Debt pretends to be
your friend

It gives you things
again and again.

Debt buys you toys
and buys you snacks

But it's not your friend
'til you pay it back.

BEST FRIENDS FOREVER

They charge
you lots
for their
magic card

And if you're late
your life gets hard.

The fun is over
you're out of luck
you've lost your hat
and now you're stuck.

MAGICARD

SQUEEZ YA

You pay your bills
with your new card

You'll owe a lot
but you can restart.

You have your stuff
and you have your house

You have red shoes
and a new white blouse.

You will ask yourself
where is my hat?

Where did I lose it?
where is it at?

You'll look a lot
you'll look on floors

You'll look in rooms
and behind doors.

When you find your hat
you'll be glad

You'll tell your mom
and tell your dad.

I have my hat
I've got it back

It once was red but
now it's black.

YOU FOUND YOUR HAT

IT FOUND

ITS HEAD!

You'll cut those cards
throw them away

The things you want
with cash you'll pay.

A smaller house
will feel just fine

With friends and love
and peace of mind.

Mitch Anthony is a leader in the education of financial services professionals and consumers about the importance of fiscal responsibility. He has been named one of the financial service industry's top "Movers & Shakers" for his efforts to bring transparency and responsibility to the industry. Mitch is the author of the popular book *The New Retirementality: Planning Your Life and Living Your Dreams…at Any Age You Want. The Cash in the Hat* is his 12th book. **www.mitchanthony.com**

Greg Wimmer is a Rochester, MN-based graphic designer and mural artist who specializes in creating designs that get people buzzing. Many of Greg's murals have become local landmarks. View his work at **www.gregsgraphicart.com**.